The Camel's Blanket

By Sally Cowan

A long time ago, Layla and her dad had a big herd of camels.

Dad sold them at the market.

People could travel across
the sand dunes on camels.

People wanted camels with big humps and long legs.

No one wanted Flea, the little brown camel.

One day, Layla had taken
Flea from his pen.

The little camel needed plants
to eat.

"You look beautiful in your blanket, Flea," Layla said.

His blanket had tiny golden bells on it.

"We should go home before that big sand storm comes!" Layla said.

But soon, the sand storm blew in!

Layla was not safe
out in the open.

The swirling sand was so thick.

She could not even see
the ground!

Layla was lost!

What could she hide behind?

Then ...

Layla followed the sound
of the golden bells.

Then she could feel Flea
beside her!

Layla crawled behind
Flea's blanket.

The storm was long, so she went
to sleep.

When Layla woke up,
the wind was still.

Layla brushed sand off
Flea's blanket.

Ting! Ting!

"There you are, Layla!"
Dad yelled.
"I tracked the bells!"

"Flea kept me safe behind
his blanket!" she said.

"You are the **best** camel, Flea!" said Layla.

"I will not sell him," said Dad. "Not even for a sack of coins!"

CHECKING FOR MEANING

1. What type of camel did people want to buy? *(Literal)*

2. How did Layla become lost? *(Literal)*

3. Why did Layla think Flea was the best camel? *(Inferential)*

EXTENDING VOCABULARY

market	What is a *market*? Have you ever been to a market? What can you buy there?
travel	What does it mean to *travel*? What are different ways you can travel? What do you travel in or on?
wanted/ needed	What is the difference between the meaning of the words *wanted* and *needed*? How is it different to want something than to need it?

MOVING BEYOND THE TEXT

1. Find out some of the special features camels have that help them to survive in the desert.

2. Which other animals sometimes have a rug to wear when the weather is cold? How do other animals keep warm in the winter?

3. Have you ever been in a sandstorm? Where were you? What did you do to stay safe?

4. Talk about the purpose of little bells on a cat's collar. Why are they there? What happens when they run or pounce?

THE SCHWA

a	e	i	o	u

PRACTICE WORDS

Layla

a

ago

across

camels

the

travel

taken

golden

even

open

blanket

market

camel

The